Nifast
Infection Prevention and Control

Infection Prevention and Control

FETAC Level 5

Nifast

Gill & Macmillan

Gill & Macmillan
Hume Avenue
Park West
Dublin 12
www.gillmacmillan.ie

© Nifast 2013

978 07171 5729 7

Print origination by Síofra Murphy
All images courtesy of Shutterstock and Presenter Media
Printed by GraphyCems, Spain

Contents

Chapter 3 Healthcare Associated Infections

Chapter 4 Health Management

Chapter 1

Basic Microbiology

Chapter Outline

- List the various types of micro-organisms.
- Describe the elements required for microbial growth.
- Describe how micro-organisms multiply and spread, and the subsequent infection process.
- List the ways in which micro-organisms spread.
- Describe what is meant by direct and indirect contact.
- Understand what is meant by resident and transient micro-organisms.
- Understand the Chain of Infection.
- Briefly describe sources of potential infection within your own workplace.
- Understand the importance of patient susceptibility and the need for vigilance and safe practice at all times.
- Understand how to eradicate micro-organisms from the environment.

- Explain the term 'antibiotic resistance' and understand the importance of correct and safe antibiotic usage.

Microbiology

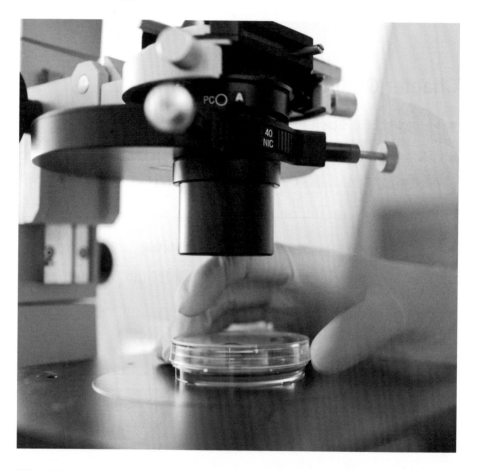

Microbiology is the study of tiny living things called micro-organisms. Micro-organisms include bacteria, viruses and fungi, and are found everywhere, for example in and on people and animals, and in water, soil, food and air. Most micro-organisms are not harmful and live in and on the human body without causing any harm. Many play a valuable role in digestion and in protecting the body against invasion by other harmful micro-organisms.

Common uses of micro-organisms:

1. Moulds are used in the manufacture of antibiotics (e.g. penicillin).
2. Some bacteria are used to make cheese and yoghurts.
3. Viruses are used in medical research.
4. Yeast is used in the manufacture of beer.

Pathogens

Micro-organisms can also be harmful and a few species are capable of causing disease when they enter the body. This may include a minor infection which stays in one part of the body or spreads throughout the body like flu. Some infections are easily dealt with but others may sometimes cause serious problems. Micro-organisms that are able to invade the body and cause disease are called pathogens and the capacity of a micro-organism to cause disease is referred to as pathogenicity.

Pathogens can be present on the body without invading tissue or causing infection. This is known as **colonisation**. Colonisation has no adverse effect on the individual concerned but it provides a source from which the pathogen can be readily transferred to another person and subsequently cause infection.

Opportunistic Pathogens

Some pathogens will cause infection if they gain access to the human body, but the severity of the disease may depend on the vulnerability of the host, such as the elderly, very young, immunocompromised and pregnant women. For example, the bacteria Shigella causes dysentery, an acute diarrhoeal illness, which tends to be most serious in debilitated individuals. Other micro-organisms are only able to cause disease in individuals with impaired defences and these are known as opportunistic pathogens. Methicillin-resistant Staphylococcus aureus, more commonly known as MRSA, may be described as an opportunistic pathogen as those at greatest risk are older people; very young people; those with reduced immunity to infection (including people living with HIV or undergoing anti-cancer therapies); those who have had surgery recently; and long-term residents of healthcare facilities.

Types of Micro-organisms

Micro-organisms include bacteria, viruses and fungi (moulds and yeasts).

Bacteria

Bacteria are very tiny living things which are too small to be seen by the naked eye and can only be viewed under a microscope. They come in three main shapes – spiral shaped, rod shaped and spherical shaped. In the healthcare environment microbiological hazards must be reduced to a safe level in order to avoid the spread of infection and disease. Common healthcare associated bacterial infections are MRSA, Clostridium difficile (C. diff.), legionnaire's disease (Legionella), Pseudomonas aeruginosa, vancomycin-resistant Enterococcus (VRE) and tuberculosis (TB). Bacterial hazards in the kitchen include Escherichia coli (E. coli), Salmonella, Listeria and Campylobacter.

In order to prevent the growth and multiplication of pathogenic bacteria, it is necessary to understand the requirements for bacterial growth. Just like all other living creatures, bacteria need food and water to grow and multiply. Most will not survive for long on clean, dry surfaces but will readily multiply on poorly cleaned equipment, in dirty water and even in solutions of disinfectant.

In a process known as binary fission, bacteria will split in two approximately every 20 minutes under the right conditions. This is known as an asexual form of reproduction as it does not involve both a male cell and a female cell. Each cell will produce an identical cell which in turn will split in two if conditions remain favourable. The requirements for bacterial growth are time, warmth, oxygen, food and moisture (TWOFM).

1. *Time*: In a 10-hour period one single cell of bacteria will become 1 billion bacterial cells if the conditions are right.

2. *Warmth*: For each species of bacteria there is a definite range within which growth takes place. Some will grow very well at room temperature or even body temperature (37°C).

3. *Oxygen*: Some bacteria are aerobic (they need oxygen to survive) and others are anaerobic (they can survive in the absence of oxygen).

4. *Food*: Like humans, bacteria require food to thrive and grow.

5. *Moisture*: Bacteria require moist conditions in order to multiply. Bacteria will not multiply on dry surfaces or equipment.

Viruses

Viruses differ from bacteria in that they are much smaller in size and are too small to be seen under an ordinary light microscope. They are also more difficult to kill. However, the main difference between viruses and bacteria is the way in which they reproduce. Viruses cannot reproduce by themselves as bacteria do and can only replicate inside a living cell; therefore, they are dependent on the host cell for growth. They can infect plants, animals and even bacteria and are responsible 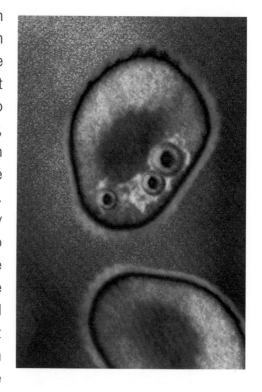 for a wide range of infections. Common healthcare associated viruses include norovirus, hepatitis B, hepatitis C and HIV (human immunodeficiency virus).

Fungi

Fungi are another type of micro-organism. Some fungi, like mushrooms, are visible to the naked eye and others can only be seen under a micro-scope. Infection caused by fungi, called mycosis, can be superficial and affect body surfaces, for example skin, hair and

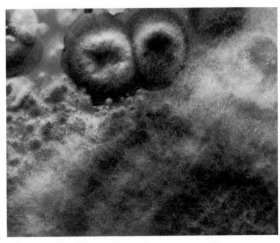

nails; these include athlete's foot, thrush and ringworm. However, in those with a compromised immune system, fungal infections (for example, Aspergillus) can invade the lungs and other tissues of the body and can very often be fatal.

Spores

Some species of bacteria develop highly resistant structures called spores when they are exposed to adverse conditions. Spores are resistant to disinfectants as well as to high and low temperatures. They may remain viable for several years, but when the environmental conditions improve, the spores germinate and the bacterial cell inside

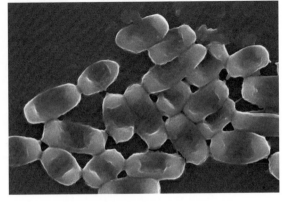

starts to multiply again. Bacterial spores can survive in dust for long periods of time, for example in the case of C. diff. Environmental contamination from C. diff. patients has been positively identified as the source of infection in reported outbreaks in healthcare settings.

Spread of Micro-organisms

In the healthcare environment micro-organisms can be spread either directly or indirectly.

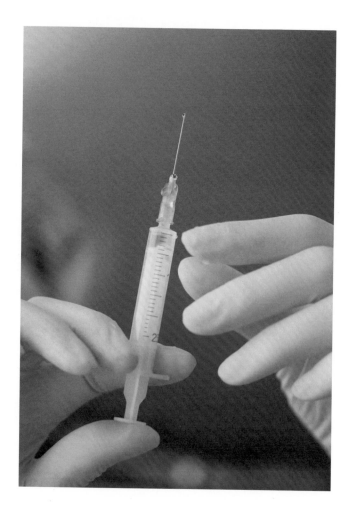

Direct contact is when micro-organisms are transferred from one infected person to another by direct contact between body surfaces, for example through the blood, other bodily fluids or sexual contact. Puncture wounds from sharps (needles, syringes and razor blades) that have been contaminated by blood from an infected patient can lead to viral infections, such as hepatitis B and hepatitis C which both cause inflammation of the liver. HIV can also be contracted through needle stick injury from an infected patient.

Indirect contact involves the transfer of a micro-organism by means of a vehicle i.e. a contaminated object or equipment (fomites). Micro-organisms can be indirectly transferred by means of the following vehicles.

Hands

Healthcare assistants can carry pathogenic bacteria on their hands through contact with contaminated surfaces or bodily fluids and these can be transferred to the next person or object that they touch. The spread of pathogenic bacteria in this manner can be easily prevented by carrying out the correct level of hand hygiene.

Equipment and Inanimate Objects

Micro-organisms can be carried on equipment such as wheels of trolleys, wheelchairs, cleaning equipment and beds, and other inanimate objects such as door handles, telephones, wash basins, taps and other unclean surfaces.

Airborne Particles

Pathogenic micro-organisms can be carried on airborne particles such as respiratory droplets, water and dust. Droplets of moisture are expelled from the respiratory tract during sneezing, coughing or talking and can be carried through the air.

Vectors

Animals and insects carry harmful bacteria on their feet, coats, fur and bodies and are very often involved in the transmission of infection to humans.

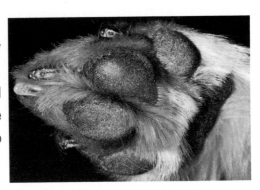

Food and Water

Some foods either in their ready-to-eat or raw state will harbour pathogenic bacteria which can cause food poisoning when consumed by vulnerable patients. Common food poisoning bacteria include Salmonella, E. coli, Listeria and Campylobacter. Food workers suffering from gastrointestinal infection should not work with food as harmful bacteria can be transmitted via the hands to patients and co-workers. Micro-organisms can also be transmitted through contaminated water as in the case of Cryptosporidium. Hepatitis A is an example of a waterborne illness, which is associated with countries that have poor sanitation and hygiene standards.

Transient and Resident Micro-organisms

Transient micro-organisms are found on the skin's surface and live for only a short period of time. They can be easily passed from one person to another and cause infection unless removed. Transient micro-organisms may be carried on the hands of healthcare assistants and also on equipment; thus, they are commonly connected to healthcare associated infections (HCAIs). The correct level of hand hygiene removes the risk of HCAIs.

Resident micro-organisms live much deeper in the skin or in the nose and most are harmless. They are part of our immune system, protecting us from infection, and they are not normally associated with HCAIs. They can, however, cause infection in patients who are vulnerable to infection.

What Is Infection?

An infection is an invasion of harmful micro-organisms into the body resulting in illness and disease. Transmission of micro-organisms can be via the faecal-oral route, vehicles (for example, equipment), droplets, non-human carriers, blood, bodily fluids and air.

Micro-organisms can enter the body and from here they will grow and multiply, and signs and symptoms of infection will become apparent. In order for infection to occur, a series of events must happen. This series of events is known as the Chain of Infection. There are six links in the Chain of Infection and each link must connect for an infection to occur. In the healthcare environment the aim is to break the Chain of Infection to stop infection from occurring.

Chain of Infection

To break the Chain of Infection it is important to first understand each link and how they connect to cause infection in the host.

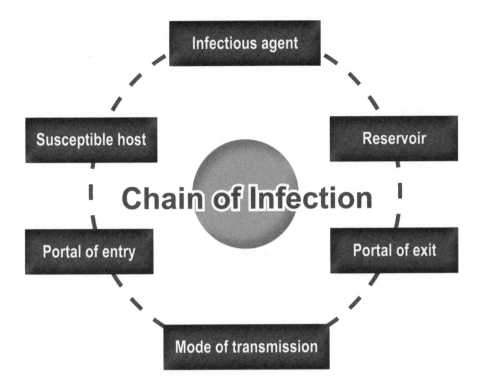

1. *Infectious agent*: This can be a bacterium, virus, fungus or parasite. Basically, any micro-organism is capable of causing infection if all the links are present. Micro-organisms are found everywhere in the environment and also on human and animal carriers.

2. *Reservoir*: This is the place where an infectious agent lives and reproduces in such a manner that it can be easily transmitted. A reservoir can be people, water, food, animals or insects.

3. *Portal of exit*: This is the means by which the infectious agent leaves the host. This can be through the respiratory tract (coughing, sneezing and talking), gastrointestinal tract (vomiting and diarrhoea), non-intact skin (draining wounds etc.) or mucous membranes (eyes, nose and mouth).

4. *Mode of transmission*: This is the way in which the micro-organisms travel from the reservoir to the host. The mode of transmission can be either direct or indirect (via a vehicle).

5. *Portal of entry*: This is the point where the infectious agent enters a new host. This process is facilitated by the respiratory tract, gastrointestinal tract, non-intact skin or mucous membranes. It can also be introduced through exposure to a contaminated sharp object like a needle or syringe (parenteral).

6. *Susceptible host*: This is the person who is about to become infected by the infectious agent. Individuals who have never been exposed to the micro-organism can become ill because they do not have the antibodies to protect them, either through immunisation or through previous infection. Certain groups are considered more vulnerable to infection and these include the elderly, the very young, pregnant women and those with underlying health problems.

The Chain of Infection can be broken in the following ways:

- Correct hand washing technique
- Segregation of healthcare linen
- Segregation of healthcare risk and non-risk waste
- Control of dust
- Cleaning of equipment and environmental cleaning

- Use of appropriate personal protective equipment (PPE)

- Pest control.

Sources of Potential Infection and Patient Susceptibility

The body has a range of defences designed to protect it against invasion by pathogens. For example, intact skin cannot be penetrated by micro-organisms but they can gain entry via damaged skin; the respiratory tract is protected by cilia (fine hair-like structures) and the cough reflex. If these defences are damaged, micro-organisms may gain access more easily.

Patients are particularly vulnerable to infection if they have pre-existing conditions. Patients receiving treatments of steroids and chemotherapy will have a lowered immune system which can affect the body's ability to deal with infection. Other underlying conditions include diabetes, renal disease, nutritional diseases (caused by malnutrition), mobility issues and general ill health. Skin lesions (wounds, burns, ulceration etc.) will also assist pathogenic micro-organisms to bypass the body's natural defences and this may lead to infection in the host.

Antibiotic Resistance

The terms **sensitive** and **resistant** are used to distinguish when a micro-organism is susceptible to or unaffected by a particular antibiotic. A sensitive micro-organism is killed, or its growth inhibited by the drug, while a resistant one survives in its presence. Antibiotic resistance is the ability of a micro-organism to withstand the effects of an antibiotic.

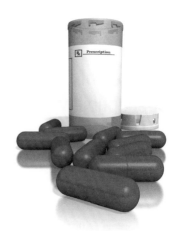

Resistance to antibiotics is increasing in many pathogens, and the unnecessary and inappropriate use of antibiotics has been recognised as a widespread and international problem for many years. At the present time MRSA and VRE are causing particular concern in the healthcare sector.

The most common abuse and misuse of antibiotics are:

1. Physicians prescribing antibiotics for viral infections.

2. Not finishing the full dosage of the antibiotic. When an antibiotic prescription is not finished (even leaving one or two pills), it leaves some bacteria alive and resistant to future antibiotic treatment.

Patients often demand that doctors prescribe antibiotics when they are not needed. Healthcare professionals must ensure that antibiotics are only prescribed when a bacterial infection is present as they are not effective against viral infections.

Revision Questions

1. List three types of micro-organisms. Name one benefit and one harm caused by each micro-organism.

2. Distinguish between 'direct' and 'indirect' contact in the spread of micro-organisms. Give two examples of each type of contact.

3. What is the main difference between bacteria and viruses?

4. List the six links in the Chain of Infection. Give a brief description of each link.

5. Briefly describe potential sources of infection within your own workplace.

Chapter 2

Basic Principles of Infection Control

Chapter Outline

- Understand the basic principles of infection control.

- Explain the importance of good hand hygiene practices and the different types of hand hygiene to be utilised.

- Explain the importance and correct use of alcohol hand gels and the need for good personal skin care.

- Understand the correct use of personal protective equipment (PPE).

- Understand what is meant by the terms cleaning, disinfection and sterilisation.

- Outline the importance of cleaning standards, correct cleaning procedures and cleaning frequencies.

- Identify the correct procedure for environmental cleaning and the decontamination of all equipment.

- Demonstrate an understanding of appropriate management of blood and bodily fluid spillages.

- Explain the difference between healthcare risk waste and healthcare non-risk waste.

- Outline the procedures for safe management and disposal of all healthcare waste.

- Describe the procedure to be followed in the event of accidental exposure to blood and bodily fluids.

- Outline the correct method for segregation of all linen.

- Understand the need for the correct storage and management of healthcare linen and the local colour-coding system in place.

Hand Hygiene

Hand hygiene is the process of cleaning the hands by following a series of simple steps. According to the Health Service Executive (HSE) (2013), hand washing is the most important and effective method in preventing the spread of healthcare associated infections (HCAIs). The hands of healthcare staff contain both transient micro-organisms and resident micro-organisms. Inadequate hand hygiene can increase the risk of transmission of transient micro-organisms which have been acquired through contact with patients, staff, contaminated equipment and the work environment. When working in any healthcare setting, it is essential that correct hand hygiene techniques are utilised at all times.

Prior to carrying out the correct hand washing technique, the following points must be adhered to: (a) fingernails must be kept clean and short; (*b*) cuts must be covered with a waterproof plaster; and (*c*) jewellery, for example rings with stones, and wrist watches, must not be worn.

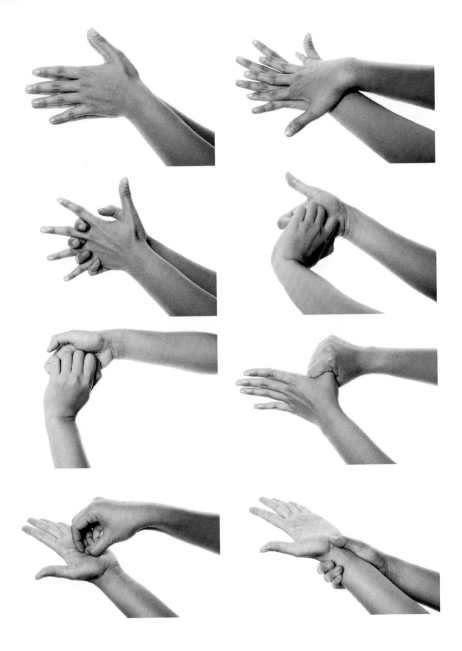

When to wash hands:

- If hands look dirty or feel sticky.
- Before and after each contact with a client.
- After taking a client's blood pressure, dressing wounds or tending catheters.
- Having handled bedpans, commodes or incontinence wear.
- Before putting on and after taking off gloves or aprons.
- After using the toilet, blowing one's nose, covering a sneeze or smoking.
- Having changed a child's nappy.
- Before and after eating or preparing food.
- Having handled raw meat.
- After handling dirty equipment or materials.
- At the beginning and end of the work shift.

Requirements for hand hygiene:

1. Use the right amount of liquid soap and warm water.
2. Use the standard technique.
3. Spend the correct amount of time (minimum 15–20 seconds).
4. Use good-quality disposable paper towels to pat hands and wrists dry.

SARI Guidelines

The SARI (Strategy for the Control of Antimicrobial Resistance in Ireland) guidelines for hand hygiene (2005) have set out three different levels of hand hygiene which are to be utilised in the healthcare environment. These are social, antiseptic and surgical hand hygiene.

Social hand hygiene is used to remove dirt, organic material, dead skin and most transient micro-organisms from the hands. It can be used following most daily tasks and involves washing the hands with a liquid soap and warm water. If the hands are visibly clean, an alcohol hand gel or rub may also be used.

Antiseptic hand hygiene is used where a higher level of cleanliness ⟨*catherisation – Dressing a wound*⟩ obtained from social hand hygiene is required, for example if a client is immunocompromised. When carried out correctly, it will remove most transient micro-organisms. It involves cleaning the hands with an alcohol hand gel or rub. This technique should only be used when the hands are visibly clean. An antiseptic liquid soap can also be used to wash hands to achieve antiseptic hand hygiene.

Surgical hand hygiene is used before all surgical procedures and removes all transient and resident micro-organisms. This level of hand hygiene is rarely required within community settings.

PRACTICAL SESSION

Hand hygiene

Demonstration and assessment of correct hand hygiene technique, including the use of alcohol gels.

Use of Personal Protective Equipment

Personal protective equipment (PPE) involves the use of gloves, apron, eye protection and face mask. They are used to protect staff and to reduce the spread of micro-organisms within the work environment. Some bodily excretions are heavily contaminated with pathogenic bacteria and present a significant risk of infection. Also, exposure to blood, tissues and bodily fluids may result in the transmission of blood-borne viruses. Protective clothing must be worn to prevent skin becoming contaminated with pathogens and to reduce the risk of their transmission to staff or via staff to patients.

Gloves

Clean disposable gloves should be readily available in all healthcare settings. Gloves are used to protect hands from getting soiled and from picking up micro-organisms, and also to reduce the risk of spreading micro-organisms to a client or other  staff. Gloves should not be worn unnecessarily as overuse may cause adverse reactions and skin sensitivities.

Catheter; Fine hollow tube used to Remove or insert fluids to and from the body.

Chapter 2 Basic Principles of Infection Control

The following are some examples of when gloves should be worn: (*a*) inserting or removing catheters; (*b*) emptying or removing urinary drainage bags; (*c*) dressing wounds; (*d*) cleaning blood or other bodily fluid spillages; and (*e*) all activities that carry a risk of blood or bodily fluids getting onto the hands.

Important points to remember:

1. Disposable gloves must be put in the correct bin after each use.

2. Disposable gloves must never be washed for reuse and must be changed between caring for different clients, or between different care activities for the same client.

3. Gloves must never be used as a substitute for hand hygiene.

4. Hands must be cleaned before putting on and after taking off gloves.

5. Always decontaminate hands after gloves are removed.

Note: Healthcare assistants suffering from hypersensitivity to latex gloves can avail of alternatives currently on the market.

Household gloves should be worn for household duties; they offer more protection than disposable gloves and, as they come further up the arm, they prevent water coming into contact with skin. Household gloves can be worn when cleaning sanitary areas like toilets, bathrooms and shower rooms; segregating routine laundry; and cleaning table tops, furniture, kitchen areas etc.

Each staff member must have their own dedicated pair of household gloves in the appropriate size. Prior to removing household gloves, they must be washed under running water using a liquid soap and left to dry in a clean area. Hands must always be cleaned on removing household gloves.

Aprons

Disposable aprons should be worn where a uniform or clothing is likely to get contaminated with blood or bodily fluids. Disposable aprons are single-use items only. They should be removed before leaving the client's room or house and disposed of in the appropriate waste bin. Hand hygiene must always be carried out after the removal of a disposable apron.

Face Protection

Face protection involves the use of protective eyewear and/or a mask. Eye protection should be used when providing care to a client where there is a risk of blood or bodily fluids splashing into the eyes. In certain circumstances face masks will be required for respiratory protection, for example if a client has a serious infectious respiratory disease, such as pulmonary tuberculosis (TB), pandemic flu or SARS.

Hand hygiene must be performed after the removal of any face protection to ensure that hands have not become contaminated on their removal.

Procedure for Removing PPE

When removing PPE, the correct procedure is as follows:

1. Untie the apron by carefully pulling on the end of the ties at the back, taking care not to touch the inner clothing.

2. Place the hands on the outside of the apron and pull downward to remove both the apron and the gloves in one movement, ensuring that you only touch the inside of the apron with your bare hands.

3. Continue to carefully roll the apron into a ball and place the waste into a healthcare risk bag.

4. Perform hand hygiene.

5. To remove eye protection, handle by head band or ear pieces, and place in a healthcare risk waste bag.

6. If a face mask has been used, remove the face mask from the bottom, then grasp by top ties or elastics, and carefully dispose of it into the healthcare risk waste bag.

7. Perform hand hygiene.

Decontamination of Equipment

Equipment used by clients can become contaminated with blood, bodily fluids or micro-organisms during the delivery of care. It is important to ensure that equipment is cleaned so that infection is not spread from equipment to people. This can happen via hand contact and during normal use.

Client equipment should be decontaminated as follows:

1. After each use.

2. When visibly dirty.

3. On a scheduled routine basis as detailed by local policy. Generally, this will be after each use, on a daily basis or when it is considered a risk.

4. Immediately when spillages of or contamination by blood or bodily fluid has occurred.

5. When a client is discharged.

The National Hospitals Office (NHO) (2006) under the HSE has outlined three levels of decontamination which must be adhered to in the healthcare environment:

1. *Cleaning*: A process that physically removes contamination but does not necessarily destroy micro-organisms.

2. *Cleaning followed by disinfection*: A process that reduces the number of viable micro-organisms but which may not inactivate some bacterial spores.

3. *Cleaning followed by sterilisation*: A process that renders an object free from viable micro-organisms, including viruses and bacterial spores.

In order to determine the level of decontamination required, the following risk assessment can be used as a guide.

Risk Assessment Decontamination Method

Risk	Application of Item	Recommendation
HIGH	• In close contact with a break in the skin or mucous membrane *or* • For introduction into sterile body areas	Sterilisation
INTERMEDIATE	• In contact with mucous membranes *or* • Contaminated with particularly virulent or readily transmissible organisms *or* • Prior to use on immunocompromised patients	Sterilisation or disinfection required
LOW	• In contact with healthy skin *or* • Not in contact with the patient	Cleaning

Source: National Hospitals Office/Health Service Executive 2006

Cleaning Policies and Procedures

The NHO/HSE (2006) has outlined the correct procedures for cleaning and disinfection in the healthcare environment.

Best practice for general cleaning:

1. Refer to in-house policy for guidance on all cleaning processes, cleaning frequencies, colour coding, protective clothing, cleaning solutions etc.

2. For all cleaning materials and equipment, always refer to manufacturers' instructions.

3. Cleaning equipment used must be safe and appropriate for each application.

4. Ensure that all equipment is clean and dry before starting procedure.

5. Plan work route and, when necessary, remove furniture and equipment.

6. Always use clean hazard-warning signs. Position them at the start of the task where they will be most effective so that people will know cleaning is in progress. Remove, clean and return them to the storage area when the task is complete and the floor is dry.

7. When cleaning or using cleaning equipment, items must be checked for damage or wear which would impair future use or endanger the safety of any individual. If damaged, do not use the equipment and report the damage to the supervisor.

8. When using electrical equipment, a circuit breaker should be used.

9. When operating electrical equipment, always keep the cable behind the machine.

10. Do not adjust or change the fittings on a machine when it is plugged in.

11. Wear goggles while preparing cleaning solutions. Goggles should be worn during processes when there is a likelihood of splashing.

12. For health and safety reasons, always add the cleaning agent to water to prevent the possibility of the cleaning agent being splashed into the eyes.

13. Never mix cleaning agents as poisonous gases could result.

14. Always ventilate areas where chemicals are being used.

15. A general cleaning rule is to start cleaning at the highest point and work towards the lowest/from outside to inside/from the cleanest area to the dirtiest area.

Colour Coding of Cleaning Equipment

Colour coding of cleaning equipment is necessary to avoid cross-contamination. This system relates to all cleaning equipment, cloths and gloves.

SANITARY APPLIANCES
AND WASHROOM
FLOORS

GENERAL LOWER
RISK AREAS
(excluding food areas)

GENERAL FOOD AND
BAR USE

WASH BASINS AND OTHER
WASHROOM SURFACES

Red signifies all cloths and equipment for use in sanitary areas, for all sanitary appliances and for the washroom floor. It is essential that two colours be used in the washroom/sanitary area.

Blue is the colour for all cloths and equipment for all general areas, for example departmental areas, office areas, public areas etc.

Yellow is the nominated colour for wash hand basins and all other washroom surfaces.

Green is the colour for all kitchens.

Cleaning Equipment

Dust Control – Damp Dusting

In order to control dispersal of dust, and in line with the NHO/ HSE guidelines (2006) on cleaning for acute hospitals, only damp dusting should be carried out in the healthcare environment. Dry dusting is not recommended. Damp dusting is to be carried out on the following surfaces: residents' beds, residents' trolleys, bedside lockers, equipment trolleys and cleaning equipment.

Mop Sweeping

Due to the likelihood of dispersal of dust, sweeping brushes are prohibited in resident settings and clinical areas. A mop sweeper (dust control device) is to be utilised at all times.

Damp Mopping – Flat Mopping System

To reduce the risk of cross-contamination, a flat mopping system, using microfibre mop heads, has been introduced which assists in eliminating the hazards associated with a conventional mopping system. Microfibre mops are recognised as being an effective infection control tool in the healthcare sector due to their ability to break

up surface dirt and remove oils and other grimy substances from floors and other surfaces.

Traditional mopping systems involved washing the mop head in a disinfectant solution and letting it dry overnight, which provided ideal conditions for bacterial growth. The flat mopping system allows the cleaning operative to detach the mop head at the end of a task and send it to laundry to be washed and dried under hygienic conditions. Starting off with dry equipment at the beginning of the day ensures that the risk of cleaning with contaminated equipment has been eliminated.

Note: Always refer to colour-coding policy for cleaning equipment when using the flat mopping system.

Sanitary Cleaning

In the healthcare environment cleaning of washrooms/bathrooms causes particular problems in relation to infection control issues. The washroom environment is a breeding ground for bacteria and extreme caution must be exercised to ensure that cleaning techniques utilised are not contributing to cross-contamination of other areas. Washroom equipment to be cleaned on a daily basis includes the following: toilets, baths, showers, wash hand basins, and washroom floors and walls.

Important points to remember:

1. Colour-coding system of cleaning equipment must be strictly adhered to when cleaning washroom areas.

2. Two colours must be always in operation – one for cleaner areas and one for dirty areas (e.g. toilets).

3. Always clean from cleanest area to dirtiest area.

4. Ensure dedicated cleaning equipment is used for isolation rooms.

5. Always remove PPE and wash hands when moving from one washroom area to another.

Healthcare Waste

Healthcare waste is the solid or liquid waste arising from healthcare and can be either non-risk waste or risk waste. The majority is non-risk domestic waste and can be carefully disposed of as household waste.

Healthcare Non-Risk Waste

Healthcare non-risk waste can be categorised as follows: domestic waste; medical equipment that is assessed as non-infectious; potentially offensive material; or confidential material.

Domestic waste includes normal household and catering waste that cannot be recycled. It is waste that is non-infectious, non-toxic, non-radioactive and non-chemical. Examples include general everyday items like food and packaging. Domestic waste such as waste food can be composted if facilities are available.

Medical equipment in this sense includes equipment that has been assessed as non-infectious. This means that it has not been contaminated with blood or bodily fluids. Items in this category include oxygen face masks, empty urine catheter drainage bags, empty enteral feed bags, and disposable gloves and aprons.

Potentially offensive material includes incontinence wear from non-infected clients and stoma bags that have not been soiled with blood. This material is deemed to be non-infectious.

Confidential material includes shredded waste paper and documents of a confidential nature. Most waste paper can be recycled so before disposing of this waste into the black bin, check to see if it could actually be disposed of in the dry recycling bin.

Healthcare Risk Waste

A small proportion of healthcare waste is potentially hazardous, or risk waste. This is due to the risk of it being infectious to those who come into contact with it or because it contains used sharp materials that could cause injury. The Department of Health and Children's guidelines for healthcare risk waste (2004) define potentially offensive infectious waste and outline the precautions to be taken when handling and storing risk waste. Risk waste can include general risk waste, chemical (healthcare) risk waste and sharps.

General risk waste includes blood, and items that are soiled with blood, for example dressings, swabs, bandages, gloves and aprons. It also includes incontinence wear from clients who have a known or suspected enteric infection, for example salmonella, C. diff or

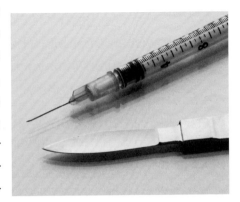

norovirus. Items contaminated with bodily fluids other than faeces, urine or breast milk are also categorised as general risk waste. ***Chemical (healthcare) risk waste*** includes discarded chemicals and medicines. ***Sharps*** are objects that have been used in the treatment of a client and that are likely to cause a puncture wound or cut to the skin. Examples include syringes, needles, scalpels and razor blades.

Disposal of Healthcare Risk Waste

There are a number of different types of risk waste bags and boxes used in the community setting. However, all bins are coloured yellow with colour-coded lids to represent their different uses.

- A yellow bag is used for bloodstained or contaminated items that are soft. Examples include soiled dressings, swabs, bandages, gloves and incontinence waste from clients that are known or suspected to have an enteric infection.

- A yellow rigid box with a yellow lid is used to dispose of contained blood and bodily fluids, for example vacuum dressings, suction machine liners, dialysis equipment and sputum containers.

- A yellow rigid box with a purple lid is used to dispose of chemicals and medicines from a pharmacy.

- A yellow sharps bin with a blue lid or red lid should be used for sharp items such as needles, syringes, scalpels and stitch cutters.

- A yellow sharps bin with a purple lid is used to dispose of sharps such as the intravenous administration sets, needles and syringes that have been used for the administration of cytotoxic drugs.

Biohazard Bags

Bloodstained or contaminated items, including dressings, swabs and bandages from infected clients, and PPE (gloves, aprons and gowns) used by staff members when attending to infected residents, must be disposed of in the following manner:

1. All items to be placed in a yellow biohazard bag – do not overfill.

2. Bags must be securely closed with cable tie or tape when two-thirds full maximum.

3. When securely tied, bags must be removed to designated area.

4. Bags must not be used for sharp or breakable items or for liquids.

Safe Handling of Sharps

The Department of Health and Children (2004) define sharps as 'any object that has been used in the diagnosis, treatment or prevention of disease that is likely to cause a puncture wound or cut to the skin'. Sharps injuries

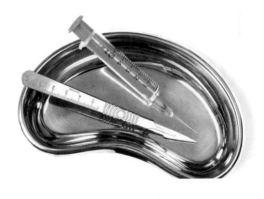

can include puncture of the skin by a needle, syringe, broken glass or razor which has become contaminated by blood from an infected patient.

When handling sharps, adhere to the following procedures:

1. Avoid the use of sharps if possible.

2. All staff who handle sharps should be immunised against hepatitis B.

3. Sharps containers in use must comply with national and international standards (UN 3291, BS 7320).

4. Sharps containers must be assembled correctly and must have an identification label.

5. Sharps containers should be available at the point of use.

6. When transporting a used syringe (e.g. arterial blood sampling), remove the needle using a removal device and attach a blind hub prior to transportation.

7. Avoid re-sheathing needles manually and re-sheath as a last resort.

8. To re-sheath safely, place sheath on a flat surface. Only re-sheath needles if a device is available to allow this to be done using one hand only.

9. Do not pass sharps from hand to hand. Use kidney dish/tray.

10. When using sharps during a procedure, ensure that they do not become obscured by dressings, paper towelling, drapes etc.

Note: Ask for assistance when taking blood or giving injections to uncooperative or confused clients.

Safe Disposal of Sharps

1. Inspect the refuse bag before removal/transport in case of inappropriate disposal of sharps.

2. Never discard needles, syringes or sharps in a polythene bag.

3. Discard sharps into a sharps container at the point of use immediately following use.

4. Discard disposable syringes and needles wherever possible as a single unit into sharps containers.

5. Sharps such as small quantities of broken glass, drug vials, used needles and razor blades must be carefully disposed of into approved sharps containers.

6. Never attempt to decant contents of small sharps containers into larger containers.

7. Never dispose of sharps into containers used for storage of other waste, or place used sharps containers in clinical waste bags.

8. Never leave sharps lying around.

9. Never insert fingers/hand past the level of the lid on a sharps container.

10. Close the aperture on the disposal of each sharp at the client's bedside.

11. Ensure sharps containers are free from protruding sharps.

12. Sharps containers should not be filled above the fill line. Replace when three-quarters full.

13. Once full, the container aperture is locked. Then the sharps container is tagged and the identification label signed.

14. The person who locks the sharps container must tag the sharps container.

Needle Stick Injury Procedure

In the event that a healthcare assistant or a staff member receives a needle stick injury, the following procedure must be adhered to:

1. Wash wound with soap under warm running water.

2. Squeeze wound to encourage bleeding.

3. All needle stick injuries must be reported to management.

4. Post-exposure, the staff member must be tested for hepatitis B, hepatitis C and HIV.

5. Monitor and retest affected staff member for blood-borne pathogens after a six-week period and again at six months.

Segregation of Healthcare Linen

Linen or laundry that has been used in a healthcare environment must be treated as a potential risk of infection and needs to be segregated appropriately. All linen can be categorised into the following three groups: clean/unused linen; dirty/used linen; and foul/infected linen.

Handling and Storage of Clean/Unused Linen

Clean/unused linen is any linen that has not been used since it was last laundered.

1. Clean/unused linen must be stored off the floor in a clean, closed cupboard and must not be stored in the sluice or bathroom.

2. Clean/unused linen must be segregated from dirty/used linen.

3. Linen cupboard doors must be kept closed to prevent airborne contamination.

4. Clean/unused linen should be delivered to wards in clean containers; these containers should not be then used to collect used linen.

5. If clean/unused linen is taken into an isolation room and not used, it must be laundered before use.

Handling of Dirty/Used Linen

All dirty linen must be handled with care to minimise the transmission of micro-organisms via dust and skin scales.

1. Plastic aprons should be worn when there is potential for contamination of clothing i.e. when changing beds.

2. Bring the laundry skip to the bedside and place dirty/used linen into the appropriate bag. All dirty/used linen must be placed carefully and directly into the appropriate laundry bag (white bag) on removal from the bed or patient/client.

3. Hands must be washed immediately following the handling of any dirty/used linen.

4. To avoid spillage of dirty/used linen, laundry bags must never be more than two-thirds full.

5. Bags must be secured appropriately for transporting to the laundry.

6. Vehicles or trolleys used to transport dirty/used linen must be easy to clean and must never be used to transport clean linen.

Handling of Foul/Infected Linen

Infected linen includes bed linen that has been soiled with blood or any other bodily fluid, or bed linen that has been used by a patient/ client with a known infection (soiled or not). All infected linen must be handled with care to minimise transmission of micro-organisms via dust and skin scales.

1. Plastic aprons and gloves must be worn when handling infected linen.

2. All infected bed linen must be placed into a water-soluble alginate stitch bag.

3. The water-soluble alginate stitch bag is then put into a red linen bag for transportation.

4. Linen bags must never be more than two-thirds full.

5. The water-soluble alginate stitch bag must be placed directly into the washing machine and not opened before washing.

6. Hands must be washed immediately following the handling of any foul or contaminated linen.

Revision Questions

1. Name three types of personal protective equipment. In each case, give an example of when they should be worn.

2. Distinguish between the terms cleaning, disinfecting and sterilising.

3. Discuss the relevant acronyms listed below and identify as many as possible:

   TB, HSE, SARI, SARS, DOHC, MRSA, TWOFM.

4. Discuss and list ten important practices in general cleaning (referring to your place of work) from the guidelines given in the NHO/HSE's *Cleaning Manual – Acute Hospitals*.

Chapter 3

Healthcare Associated Infections

Chapter Outline

- Explain the concept of healthcare associated infections.

- List the predisposing factors in the development of healthcare associated infections.

- Have a basic understanding of the main healthcare associated infections.

- List the main blood-borne viruses which pose a threat within a healthcare setting.

- Understand the need for care when handling blood and bodily fluids.

- List ways of preventing the spread of these infections (i.e. standard precautions).

- Understand what is meant by 'contact precautions', 'airborne precautions' and 'droplet precautions'.

- Understand the important role of single-use items within the healthcare setting.

- Describe what cleaning fluid is used in different situations.

- Understand the need for the correct storage and management of cleaning fluids.

- Outline how routine cleaning can affect the spread of such healthcare associated infections.

- Understand what is meant by 'terminal cleaning'.

- Outline the procedure for cleaning an 'isolation room'.

- Understand the importance of food hygiene in all healthcare settings.

According to the Centers for Disease Control and Prevention (2012) healthcare associated infections (HCAIs) are infections that clients acquire during the course of receiving healthcare treatment for other conditions. This infection would not have been present or incubating at the time of admission. If the client gets sick within the first 48 hours of having been admitted to the healthcare facility, they are likely to have brought the infection with them.

Predisposing Factors

There are certain factors that will make an individual client more susceptible to HCAIs than others. These include: (a) large wounds or burns, or recovery following surgery or a serious accident;

(*b*) being on a drip (intravenous line) or other medical devices for a long period of time; (*c*) a weakened immune system (such as patients who have been treated for leukaemia or cancer) or an organ transplant; and (*d*) extremes of age (with the very young and the elderly being more vulnerable to infection). Also, resistant strains of bacteria are more likely to prevail in the hospital environment and to spread from one person to another as a result of regular exposure to antibiotics, due to the fact that clients are more likely to receive antibiotics for infection or as prophylaxis against infection prior to and post surgery.

TASK

What is the cost of a HCAI to the client, their family and the healthcare environment?

Common HCAIs

Common HCAIs include methicillin-resistant Staphylococcus aureus (MRSA), Clostridium difficile (C. diff.), norovirus, hepatitis B and C, HIV, vancomycin-resistant Enterococcus (VRE), Escherichia coli (E. coli) and legionnaire's disease.

MRSA

Methicillin-resistant Staphylococcus aureus is a strand of Staphylococcus aureus (Staph. aureus) which has become resistant to many antibiotics commonly used to treat Staphylococcus infections. As a result of this, Staphylococcus infections can be difficult to treat. Staphylococcus aureus colonises the nose and skin of healthy people, in particular the groin and perineum. Approximately 20 per cent of people have the organism most of the time and a further 60 per cent carry it intermittently. It can cause infection if it enters damaged skin or surgical wounds and, in severe cases, can lead to septicaemia and pneumonia. Staphylococcus aureus is a major cause of infection associated with the healthcare environment.

MRSA can be carried on the hands of healthcare assistants and spread by direct skin contact with patients. Staff clothing and equipment may also be involved in the transmission but, although the organism can survive in dust for long periods of time, the environment is not considered to play an important part in transmission in most settings. Those with a weakened immune system or skin lesions/open wounds are more susceptible to MRSA than healthier members of the population.

Hand washing has been acknowledged as being the single most important factor in the fight against MRSA infections. Where possible, affected patients should be nursed in a single room and staff must ensure that correct hand hygiene techniques are utilised before and after contact with MRSA patients and their environment. Cleaning policies should be in place and careful attention must be given to the possibility of an accumulation of dust on horizontal surfaces. PPE must be worn during contact with affected patients and discarded after use.

Clostridium Difficile

Clostridium difficile is a common inhabitant of the human gut but exposure to antibiotics can allow it to multiply and disturb the balance of flora in the gut. The illness is characterised by severe bloody diarrhoea 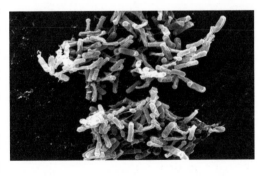 and may be fatal in some cases. The route of transmission is via direct/indirect contact with faeces and it may be carried on the hands of healthcare assistants from where it can be passed to vulnerable groups. Clostridium difficile produces spores that are resistant to many cleaning agents and can survive for prolonged periods in the environment.

Correct and frequent hand hygiene when dealing with Clostridium difficile patients is recommended to avoid the possibility of transferring the bacteria from affected patients to other persons and the environment. Effective environmental cleaning is a priority in the presence of Clostridium difficile as bacterial spores can survive in dust for long periods of time. Healthcare assistants must ensure that appropriate PPE is worn at all times when dealing with Clostridium difficile patients and discarded after use.

Norovirus

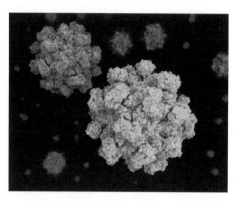 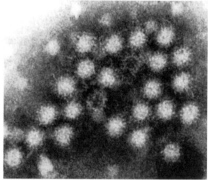

Norovirus (winter vomiting bug) is transmitted by the faecal-oral route by contaminated hands; directly from person to person; or through contaminated food or water. It can also be transmitted by contact with contaminated surfaces or fomites, for example door handles, cleaning equipment or trolleys. The infective dose of norovirus is 102 organisms in a healthy adult but can be as little as 10 organisms in those with a compromised immune system. Utilisation of the correct hand washing technique for at least 20 seconds has proven to be an effective method of preventing the spread of norovirus. Alternatively, sanitising alcohol gels can also be used, provided that hands are visibly clean.

Legionnaire's Disease

According to the HSE, there are about ten cases of legionnaire's disease reported each year. It is most common in those aged over fifty and those with a compromised immune system. Legionnaire's 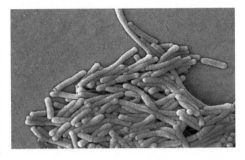 disease occurs when the bacterium Legionella (which is found in the environment) accesses a water system, for example hot and cold water distribution systems, air conditioning systems, showerheads or water fountains, and starts to multiply if conditions are right. Legionella grows well in temperatures between 20°C and 45°C and also in areas of stagnant water. Chlorination of water does not kill Legionella as it is resistant to it.

Legionnaire's disease can be contracted by inhaling droplets or spray from water systems that have become contaminated by Legionella, for example using a shower in a ward that has not been used for some time where stagnant water has been kept at optimum temperatures for bacterial growth. Legionnaire's disease is not contagious and can only be picked up from inhalation of spray or droplets that contain the bacteria. It starts with flu-like symptoms, fever, aches and pains, followed by dry cough and breathing difficulties, and it may progress to severe pneumonia.

In order to eliminate the possibility of contracting legionnaire's disease, regular cleaning and maintenance of water distribution systems is necessary. Water must be heated to a minimum of 60°C and distributed to all outlets at below 20°C or above 50°C. Water stagnation in any part of the water system should be avoided and low use sections should be washed out on a weekly basis. Particular attention should be paid to sections of buildings that are used on a periodic basis, for example closed/partially closed hospital wards and unoccupied rooms in a nursing home environment.

Blood-borne Viruses

Blood-borne viruses (BBVs) are infectious micro-organisms in human blood that can cause disease in humans. These diseases include hepatitis B, hepatitis C and HIV.

Hepatitis B

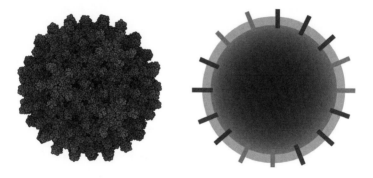

The hepatitis B disease is a potentially life-threatening liver infection caused by the hepatitis B virus (HBV). It can cause chronic liver disease and puts people at high risk of death from cirrhosis of the liver and liver cancer.

Exposure to HBV is possible through:

- Blood transfusions.

- Direct contact with blood in healthcare settings.

- Sexual contact with an infected person.

- Unclean needles or instruments used in tattooing or acupuncture.

- Needles shared in drug use.

- Personal items (such as toothbrushes, razors and nail clippers) shared with an infected person.

Many people who have chronic hepatitis B have few or no symptoms – they may not even look sick. As a result, they may not know they are infected. However, they can still spread the virus to other people. Early symptoms of the disease may include appetite loss, fatigue, low-grade fever, muscle and joint aches, nausea, vomiting, yellow skin and dark urine due to jaundice.

In the healthcare environment a hepatitis B vaccination must be offered to all staff members. All bloodstained or contaminated items, including dressings, swabs and bandages from infected patients, and PPE (gloves, aprons and gowns), must be placed in the appropriately coloured containers or bags. A safe handling and disposal of sharps policy, together with a needle stick policy, should be in place in the event of accidental exposure through puncture wounds to the skin. Appropriate PPE must be provided in conjunction with relevant staff training on the dangers of BBVs and the necessity for correct hand hygiene protocol at all times.

Hepatitis C

The hepatitis C disease is a variant of hepatitis which is caused by the hepatitis C virus (HCV). Its transmission is similar to that of HBV – in the healthcare setting the main risk is by percutaneous exposure to infected blood. It differs from HBV in that there is 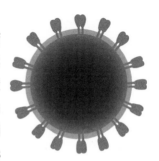 currently no vaccine for active immunisation against HCV. Control measures are similar to those of hepatitis B.

HIV

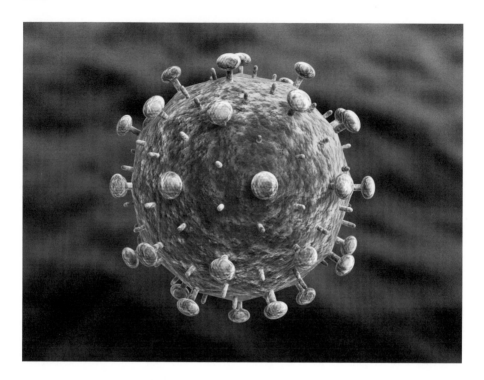

HIV is acquired through sexual contact; inoculation of blood or bodily fluids through the skin by contaminated needles or other sharp items; and exposure of mucous membranes. The virus is present in blood, semen, vaginal secretions, cerebrospinal fluid, amniotic fluid and synovial fluid. Healthcare assistants are at risk of acquiring infection through exposure to blood and bodily fluids, particularly following needle stick injury. Control measures are similar to those of other blood-borne viruses.

Tuberculosis

Tuberculosis is a contagious airborne disease which generally affects the lungs through inhalation. It is predominantly spread by coughing, sneezing, spitting or talking which expels air and disperses droplets that contain mycobacterium TB. Control measures against the spread of TB include vaccination (which should 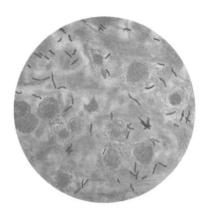 be offered to all relevant members of staff), engineering controls, administrative controls and PPE.

Engineering controls should ensure that new or refurbished healthcare settings contain isolation rooms for patients with active TB. This secluded accommodation should supply at least six air changes per hour, along with direct negative air flow coming from the corridor and exhausted to the exterior of the building to prevent the spread of TB nuclei to different parts of the building.

Administrative controls are in the form of staff training at the induction stage and at regular intervals thereafter to ensure that staff are aware of the signs and symptoms. Staff required to enter isolation rooms and come into direct contact with infectious patients must be offered additional protection. FFP1, FFP2 and FFP3 disposable face masks are to be worn as dictated by local policy. The markings FFP1, FFP2 and FFP3 offer different levels of protection – FFP3 extends the highest level of protection. These masks are wholly or substantially constructed of filtering material. Patients leaving the isolation room are also required to wear appropriate face protection. All PPE must be disposed of as per local waste management policy.

Standard Precautions

Standard precautions are a set of general infection control guidelines to be used by all healthcare staff during delivery of care to clients. They provide a foundation for infection prevention and control practices, which include: hand washing; waste management and decontamination issues; management of linen; respiratory hygiene and cough etiquette; and appropriate use of PPE.

Standard precautions aim to ensure that the Chain of Infection is not complete and to prevent the transmission of common infectious agents. Standard precautions assume infectious agents could be present in the patient's blood, bodily fluids, secretions, excretions, non-intact skin and mucous membranes.

Transmission-based Precautions

Transmission-based precautions are to be used where some transmissible infectious agents require additional controls. They are to be used in addition to the standard precautions. Organisms/ infectious agents that require additional controls include: MRSA, Clostridium difficile, TB, norovirus, H1N1 (swine flu), Salmonella, chicken pox and measles. Transmission-based precautions include the following: contact precautions, airborne precautions and droplet precautions.

Contact Precautions

'Contact precautions should be applied, in addition to standard precautions, to prevent the transmission of highly transmissible organisms that are

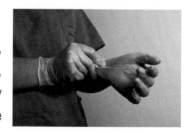

transmitted from person to person via the contact route (for example, methicillin-resistant Staphylococcus aureus).' (HSE 2007)

Contact precautions take into account both direct contact and indirect contact (via a vehicle), and contact through vectors. According to SARI (2001), the following controls should be put in place: (*a*) isolation unit/room if available; (*b*) contact the infection prevention and control team or the clinical nurse manager in charge if there is no isolation unit/room available (patient cohorting may take place); (*c*) PPE – gown and gloves for all interactions; (*d*) care of patient/client equipment; (*e*) decontamination of equipment and the environment; and (*f*) hand hygiene.

Airborne Precautions

'Airborne precautions should be applied, in addition to standard precautions, to prevent transmission of highly transmiss-ible organisms that are transmitted via the air from one person to another (for example, TB).' (HSE 2007). Airborne precautions prevent transmission of pathogens that remain infectious over long distances when suspended in the air, for example TB, measles and chicken pox.

Airborne precautions include: (*a*) airborne infection isolation room with adequate air exchanges per hour; (*b*) use of appropriate face masks as per local policy; (*c*) ensuring appropriate face mask/respirator are correctly fitted prior to entering room; (*d*) removing face mask only after leaving room; (*e*) client to wear appropriate face mask if leaving the room; and (*f*) staff training.

Droplet Precautions

'Droplet precautions should be applied, in addition to standard precautions, to prevent transmission of highly transmissible organisms that are transmitted via respiratory secretions from one person to another (for example, Influenza)' (HSE 2007). Droplet precautions are intended to prevent transmission of pathogens spread through respiratory mucous membranes.

Controls include: (*a*) a single room is preferred; (*b*) if a single room is not possible, spatial separation of more than 3 feet is required and drawing the curtain between client beds is especially important in multi-bed rooms where infections may be transmitted by the droplet route; (*c*) PPE – surgical mask if within 3 feet of the client; and (*d*) client to wear face mask when leaving the room.

Single-use Items and Reusable Items

In any healthcare environment there are two types of medical devices and equipment that will be used on a daily basis: single-use items and reusable items.

1. *Single-use items*: Examples of medical devices or equipment that carry the 'single use only' symbol include needles, syringes, scalpels and finger stick needles for blood sugar testing. The reuse of single-use devices can affect the safety, performance and effectiveness of the device, exposing clients and staff to unnecessary risk.

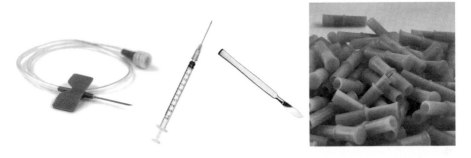

2. *Reusable items*: Reusable medical devices or equipment can be used on an on-going basis with the same or different clients, once they are cleaned appropriately after each use. Types of reusable equipment include blood pressure monitoring equipment, commodes, hoists and wheelchairs. Reusable equipment must be cleaned on a scheduled routine basis and when visibly dirty.

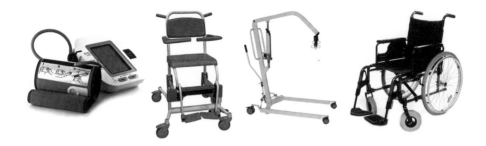

Cleaning in the Healthcare Environment

When cleaning in the healthcare environment, the healthcare assistant must be aware of the differences between cleaning, disinfection and sterilisation.

Cleaning is a process that physically removes dust and dirt – it will not kill micro-organisms. Cleaning agents (or detergents), therefore, will only remove dirt but they will not destroy any micro-organisms present on the surface. Cleaning must take place prior to disinfection.

Disinfection is a process that reduces micro-organisms to a safe level, but it does not kill all micro-organisms. For example, disinfectants may not kill bacterial spores. Disinfectants are used in the healthcare sector to deal with spillages of bodily fluids and the like. Disinfection is not effective if cleaning has not taken place beforehand. Disinfectants are only necessary to decontaminate when potential infection is suspected and after spillage of organic matter, blood, pus etc.

Sterilisation is a process that kills all micro-organisms, including viruses and bacterial spores.

TASK

Group exercise

What type of cleaning agents do you use in your organisation?

Safe Use and Storage of Cleaning Agents

When using chemicals always:

1. Follow the manufacturers' instructions.

2. Follow a cleaning schedule.

3. Remove/protect food while cleaning.

4. Use clean cleaning equipment.

5. Change cool or dirty water.

6. Report damaged equipment and low supplies of chemicals or cleaning materials.

7. Report lack of PPE.

8. Ensure a colour-coded system is in place for cleaning equipment.

9. Ensure safety data sheets are available for all chemicals.

10. Ensure cleaning chemicals are securely stored.

11. Adhere to storage instructions on labels of containers.

12. Ensure all spray bottles are cleared labelled.

Do not: (*a*) mix chemicals; (*b*) transfer chemicals to unmarked containers; (*c*) store chemicals with food; (*d*) store chemicals beside a naked flame; and (*e*) clean if you have not been trained to do so.

Cleaning Schedules

Cleaning schedules are essential to ensure that cleaning is carried out at the right time by a trained person using the correct chemicals. Cleaning schedules should state:

- What to clean.

- Who should clean.

- When to clean.

- How to clean.

- The chemical and dilution to use.

Specialist Cleaning and Deep Cleaning

In the healthcare environment there are occasions when a more specialised type of cleaning is required, for example when an isolation room has to be cleaned or terminal cleaning on a room that has been vacated by an infectious patient. These cleaning methods are undertaken to control the spread of infections.

TASK

Group exercise

What type of specialist cleaning is performed in your organisation and when is it performed? Refer to local policy for guidance.

Food Hygiene

Food hygiene is critical in the healthcare environment and food handlers must exercise extreme care when preparing and handling food that is to be served to clients. The aim of enforcing strict food hygiene standards in a healthcare setting is to prevent the possibility of clients contracting food poisoning.

Food Poisoning

Food poisoning is an illness contracted from eating contaminated food. The incubation period can be anything from 1 hour to 72 hours and the duration is usually between 1 and 7 days. The symptoms of food poisoning are abdominal pain/stomach cramps, diarrhoea, vomiting, nausea, fever, dehydration and collapse.

Certain groups are more at risk of contracting food poisoning than others. ***Vulnerable groups*** include the very young, the elderly, the immunocompromised and pregnant women. Due to varying health complications, service users of healthcare facilities are considered particularly vulnerable to food poisoning.

Food Handlers

Food handlers are considered to be all workers who handle food in the course of their work. This includes staff who cook and prepare food in the kitchen; those who reheat and serve food to clients; and those who assist clients during mealtimes. Under current legislation all food handlers have responsibilities when working with food.

As outlined by Regulation (EC) No. 852/2004 on the hygiene of foodstuffs, these responsibilities include:

1. Maintaining a high degree of personal hygiene when working with food.

2. Wearing suitable, clean and, where appropriate, protective clothing.

3. Not working with food when suffering from, or suspected to be suffering from, an illness that is likely to be transmitted through food.

4. Not working with food while afflicted with infected wounds, skin infections, vomiting or diarrhoea.

5. Reporting all illnesses to a supervisor and not working with food.

When working with food, it is essential that food handlers maintain high standards of personal hygiene at all times. Uniforms must be kept clean, and regular and adequate hand washing must be performed to ensure that pathogenic bacteria are not transferred from hands to food. Fingernails must be kept clean and short, and jewellery must not be worn, except for a plain wedding band and sleeper earrings. Uniforms must not be worn while travelling to and from work and lockers should be available for storage of outdoor clothes and personal items. All food handlers are required to have basic food hygiene training.

Food Poisoning Micro-organisms

- Salmonella – meat, eggs, poultry, and human and animal intestines
- Staphylococcus aureus – nose, throat, hair, cuts and boils
- E. coli – meat and meat products, human and animal intestines, and water
- Campylobacter – unpasteurised milk, poultry and farm animals
- Listeria – soft cheeses and paté
- Clostridium botulinum (botulism) – canned and vacuum-packed foods

Common Reasons for Food Poisoning

1. Food has been prepared too far in advance.
2. Poor personal hygiene of food handlers.

3. Poor temperature control.

4. Infected food handlers (food handlers working while sick).

5. Inadequate thawing.

6. Inadequate reheating.

7. Cross-contamination (from raw to ready-to-eat foods).

8. Inadequate segregation of food types/preparation areas.

In order to avoid contamination when working with food, it is important to wash hands:

● Before starting work.

● After touching hair, nose or face.

● After smoking, eating, coughing, sneezing and blowing the nose.

● After carrying out cleaning duties.

● After handling waste.

● After handling money.

● After handling boxes.

The healthcare assistant has a role to play in ensuring that patients or clients do not succumb to food poisoning while in their care. Adherence to good personal hygiene and the correct hand washing technique will help to reduce the possibility of patients or clients contracting this serious, and sometimes life-threatening, disease.

Revision Questions

1. List the predisposing factors in the development of healthcare associated infections.

2. List the main blood-borne viruses which pose a threat within a healthcare setting.

3. What is meant by 'contact precautions', 'airborne precautions' and 'droplet precautions'?

4. Provide two examples each of single-use items and reusable items within the healthcare setting.

5. List five specific responsibilities of all food handlers when working with food under current legislation.

Chapter 4

Health Management

Chapter Outline

- Demonstrate an awareness of the role and function of the infection control team.

- Identify how the healthcare assistant could liaise with members of their local infection control team when necessary.

- Demonstrate an awareness of both the individual's specific role and the general procedures in relation to outbreak management.

- Demonstrate an understanding of the policy on staff immunisation.

- Outline the policy with respect to wearing uniforms and jewellery.

- Demonstrate the local policy on sick leave and reporting ill health.

- Outline the policy in relation to reporting occupational injuries/issues at local level.

- Understand the importance of infection control within the built environment.

- Describe what other policies may have an impact on infection control protocol.

- Recognise the role of the healthcare assistant in preventing the spread of infection.

Role and Function of the Infection Control Team

The role and function of the infection control team in any healthcare setting is to monitor and advise on the prevention and control of infection. Preventing the spread of infection is a central principle in the structure of good health management and it is normal procedure for healthcare structures to have a 'living' infection control policy. This is a set of standards and practices that reflect the environment in which the healthcare is being delivered. This policy is constantly monitored, managed and revised to ensure safe practice in the delivery of services within a hospital or care setting. A typical frame is outlined in the following example.

Infection Prevention and Control Mission Statement, Sligo General Hospital

It is the policy of the Infection Prevention and Control Team to strive towards combating infectious diseases, in general and healthcare acquired infections in particular, by working towards ensuring the provision of the basic infrastructure to implement best practice in relation to infection prevention and control in Sligo General Hospital.

Infection Prevention and Control Team

The Infection Prevention and Control team consists of members of staff with a specialist knowledge and training in Infection Prevention and Control in the hospital setting:

- Consultant Microbiologist (who acts as the Infection Prevention and Control doctor and directs the activities of the Infection Prevention and Control Nursing Personnel)

- Assistant Director of Nursing, Infection Prevention and Control

- Clinical Nurse Manager 2

- Surveillance Scientist

The Infection Prevention and Control Team meet regularly, often on a daily basis. These individuals are also members of the Infection Prevention and Control Committee. The Infection Prevention and Control Committee is chaired by the deputy General Manager.

Source: Sligo General Hospital 2012

Liaising with Members of the Infection Control Team

Regular contact with the infection control team is necessary to ensure that any suspected infectious patients are quickly identified and essential controls are put in place to prevent the spread of infection. It is essential that the healthcare assistant is aware of the correct protocol to follow in the event that a situation has been identified which may lead to a potential outbreak.

The healthcare assistant must first report the situation to their immediate supervisor or nurse manager. Depending on the nature of the situation, the nurse manager will then decide on whether contact with the infection control team is necessary. The assistant director of nursing will normally be a member of the infection control team and can advise on the correct steps to be taken.

In a hospital situation where, for example, there is a suspected outbreak of gastrointestinal infection, the protocol would be as follows:

1.   Inform the doctor in charge of the patients.

2.   Inform the infection control doctor/nurse.

The infection control team will then decide on whether affected patients must be transferred to single rooms and isolation precautions followed. Adequate supplies of gloves and aprons must be available and staff must be aware of correct hand washing protocol at all times. The infection control team will meet on a regular basis – at least daily in the event of an outbreak. They will keep key staff members up to date on the situation and will advise on necessary precautions to be maintained until such time as the outbreak has been contained. They will also advise on the protocol to be followed in relation to visitors to the healthcare facility.

TASK

Class discussion/group work

Who is involved in your local infection control team and what is the role of each member?

How do you liaise with them?

Are the team members visible and easily accessible?

Local Policies

Immunisation Policy

Immunity is the body's defence against infection by a bacterium or virus. It develops after a person has become infected by a micro-organism or has been given a vaccine. Immunity is a long lasting defence mechanism which involves the production of antibodies that target and disable specific pathogens. Natural immunity arises when a pathogen enters the body in the normal way, for example catching a cold or flu. Artificial immunity occurs when a pathogen is medically introduced into the body, for example with vaccination.

Typical adult vaccinations include the following:

- Pneumococcal vaccine

- Influenza vaccine

- Mumps

- Hepatitis B

- Rubella

- Whooping cough.

Note: For more specific information, visit the Health Service Executive (HSE) website at http://www.immunisation.ie/en/Whoweare/.

TASK

What is the policy on immunisation in your own organisation? Are workers offered vaccinations on commencement of employment? Is health surveillance available?

Uniform and Jewellery Policy

Healthcare assistants should not wear uniforms when travelling to work. Uniforms are intended to protect service users from micro-organisms whereas outdoor clothing may harbour them. The wearing of a uniform when travelling to work will ensure that micro-organisms from outside the facility can be carried into the healthcare environment, leading to infection and illness in susceptible groups. Changing room facilities should be available for staff where they can change out of outdoor clothing prior to starting work. Lockers must be available for storage of outdoor clothing and personal items.

Jewellery should not be worn when administrating care to clients. Stones in jewellery can harbour harmful bacteria which can be transferred from healthcare assistants to clients and cause infection in high risk groups. The wearing of jewellery also inhibits correct hand washing technique.

Sick Leave and Reporting Ill Health

As the role of the healthcare assistant involves close contact with those who may be immunocompromised, early reporting of ill health is essential to ensure that it does not impact on the health of service users. In the course of their duties healthcare assistants may also be exposed to biological hazards such as hepatitis B, TB, HIV and influenza, which in turn may be passed on to clients during delivery of care if correct precautions are not implemented.

Healthcare facilities must ensure that correct protocol is in place for the reporting of ill health and that staff members are aware of the procedures to follow in the event that they contract any illness that may be easily transmissible. Personnel suffering from symptoms of diarrhoea, vomiting, gastroenteritis, influenza or skin infections should report the condition to their immediate supervisor and stay away from the workplace until they have been certified fit to return to work in a healthcare environment.

Staff members working with food must ensure that any symptoms of suspected food poisoning are promptly reported, together with gastrointestinal upsets, any infections of the mouth, nose, throat, eyes or ears, or scheduled infectious diseases including typhoid, paratyphoid, dysentery, polio or salmonella, and they must not work with food.

Healthcare assistants who have received a needle stick injury must immediately report the incident to their manager and local policy on dealing with needle stick injuries must be adhered to. Monitoring of the situation through regular blood testing must be carried out to rule out the possibility of contamination through infected bodily fluids.

The procedure for reporting of ill health will vary depending on local policy but the following can be taken as a guideline:

1. On the first day of illness the employee should contact their manager at the earliest possible convenience to advise them of their inability to attend work and the reason why.

2. When the employee is fit to resume duty, they must make contact with their manager on the day prior to returning so that the manager can make the necessary arrangements for their return.

3. Record of absences from work due to illness must be held on each individual's personnel file.

Depending on the healthcare facility, medical certification may be required after more than two consecutive days of absence and must be submitted on the third day of absence. Medical certification must be submitted thereafter on a weekly basis until such time as the employee is declared fit to return to work.

Other Policies that Impact on Infection Control Protocol

There are a number of policies that may also impact on infection control protocol.

Visitors Policy

Visitors to the healthcare facility will impact on infection control protocol so care must be taken to ensure that visitors are not a source of infection within the healthcare setting. Strict visiting times must be adhered to and visitors must be made aware that visits by those who are considered to be carriers of infectious

agents are strictly prohibited. Visitor numbers at any one time to individual patients must be curtailed and visits by children to those who are immunocompromised must be restricted. Availability of alcohol gels to facilitate hand hygiene at the entrance to healthcare facilities must be in place and clearly signposted. In the event of any outbreak within the healthcare setting, visits from members of the public must be prohibited, except for those patients who are permitted visits on compassionate grounds.

Pest Control Policy

An effective pest control policy is essential within the healthcare facility to ensure that the possibility of a pest infestation does not impact on infection control protocol. Pests (such as rats, mice, insects, flies and cockroaches) and domestic animals will carry pathogenic bacteria on their feet, bodies, skin and fur, and their presence in a healthcare setting will present a grave and immediate risk to

human health. A contract with a pest control firm must be in place which will complement infection control procedures and ensure that access by unwanted pests and pets is strictly controlled.

Food Policy

A food hygiene policy must be in place to ensure that food workers understand the importance of hygienic practices when preparing food for vulnerable groups. Food workers must be trained in basic food hygiene principles and at least one food worker must be fully trained on HACCP (Hazard Analysis and Critical Control Point) principles to ensure that correct storage methods and cooking temperatures are  adhered to at all times. Healthcare assistants who are required to handle food in the course of their work, for example assisting clients at meal times or re-heating food, must also be trained on basic food hygiene practices.

Antibiotics Policy

The use of antibiotics must be carefully monitored to ensure that the overuse of antibiotics does not contribute to the incidence of healthcare associated infections  (HCAIs). Nursing staff have an important role to play by carefully observing and recording signs and symptoms of infection and alerting medical staff to patients who may be receiving inappropriate or prolonged treatment (Wilson 2008).

Reporting Accidents

Certain accidents in the workplace need to be reported to the Health and Safety Authority (HSA). The Safety, Health and Welfare at Work (General Application) Regulations 1993 detail the workplace accidents that are reportable and these are as follows:

1. An accident resulting in a fatality of any employed or self-employed person.

2. An accident that prevented an employed or self-employed person from working for more than three calendar days (not including the day of the accident).

3. An accident caused by a work activity that caused the death, or an injury or condition requiring medical treatment, of a person not at work, for example a passer-by.

Internal Accidents

Accidents that are not required to be reported to the HSA must be recorded internally and a system should be in place for doing so. Any injuries that occur on-site must be reported by employees as soon as possible after the event and details must be recorded by a competent person. An internal investigation must be carried out, which will involve recording the exact details of the accident, interviewing witnesses and taking photographs where appropriate. Workers should also be encouraged to report incidents and near misses so that action can be taken that may prevent an accident in the future.

Always ask:

- Who do I report this to?

- When do I report it?

- How do I report it?

- Where do I report it?

- Why do I report it?

TASK

What is the system for reporting accidents in your organisation? Is there a system for reporting near misses?

Safety Representatives

Employees may select a safety representative to represent them on health and safety issues within the work environment. Under section 25 of the Safety, Health and Welfare at Work Act 2005, the safety representative has a number of rights and powers:

1. To conduct workplace inspections.

2. To carry out accident investigations.

3. To liaise with HSA inspectors.

4. Reasonable time off to attend training.

5. Must not be penalised for carrying out his/her duties.

Importance of Infection Control within the Built Environment

Infection prevention and control is critical within the built environment to ensure that service users benefit from a level of care that does not compromise health status. When examining the built environment, it must be considered that the healthcare setting is a reservoir for micro-organisms where vulnerable clients are potentially at risk of infection. In order to reduce the likelihood of contracting nosocomial infection (healthcare associated infection), environmental factors must be identified which have the potential to act as a 'vehicle' for the transfer of pathogenic bacteria.

Micro-organisms can be carried on equipment, such as wheels of trolleys, wheelchairs, cleaning equipment and beds, and other inanimate objects, such as door handles, telephones, wash hand basins, taps and other unclean surfaces. Contaminated food and water can also be potential sources of infection. The following are amongst the factors that should be considered when evaluating the built environment as a source of infection within a healthcare setting: fixtures, fittings and furniture; hand washing facilities; heating and ventilation; surfaces (worktops, ceilings and floors); waste management; and food and water.

Fixtures, Fittings and Furniture

All surfaces, fixtures and fittings should be designed to ensure easy cleaning and durability within the healthcare environment. Lighting units should be fully sealed to allow ease of cleaning and soft furnishings should be water/stain resistant and capable of withstanding disinfection with a chlorine-based disinfectant.

Any chairs and couches that are showing signs of wear and tear and are exhibiting rips and tears should be replaced to ensure that there is no risk of contamination. Curtains should be changed and washed at pre-determined schedules or when directed to do so by the infection control team.

Hand Washing Facilities

An adequate number of wash hand basins must be available and a minimum of one wash hand basin must be sited in each treatment room. All wash hand basins must be easily accessible and must not be used for any other purpose other than hand washing. Taps should be elbow or sensor operated and an adequate amount of liquid soap and alcohol gel should be available, together with disposable paper towels to facilitate drying of hands. A foot-operated bin must be located beside each wash hand basin to aid hygienic and correct disposal of waste.

Heating and Ventilation

Heating and ventilation grilles should be easily removable to facilitate cleaning them in a deep sink and radiators should be wall mounted at a high enough level to ensure that the area can be cleaned underneath.

Heating and ventilation systems, if not correctly serviced and maintained, may be a potential source of Legionella, which can lead to the development of legionnaire's disease in susceptible clients. Legionnaire's disease occurs when the bacteria Legionella, which is found in the environment, gets access to a water system (for example hot and cold water distribution systems, air conditioning systems, showerheads or water fountains) and starts to multiply under the right conditions. Wards in healthcare facilities that have been out of use for some time are particularly at risk as the bacteria may build up in the water system of shower units that have not been run on a regular basis. Stagnant water together with warm temperatures provide ideal conditions for bacterial growth.

The disease can be contracted as a result of inhaling droplets or spray from water systems that have become contaminated by Legionella. Legionnaire's disease is not contagious and can only be picked up from inhalation of spray or droplets.

In order to eliminate the possibility of contracting legionnaire's disease, regular cleaning and maintenance of water distribution systems is necessary. Water must be heated to a minimum of 60°C and distributed to all outlets at below 20°C or above 50°C. Water stagnation in any part of the system should be avoided and low use sections in water systems should be washed out on a weekly basis. Particular attention should be paid to sections of buildings that are used on a periodic basis, for example closed/partially closed hospital wards or unoccupied rooms in a nursing home environment.

Surfaces

Work surfaces should be easy to clean and adequate space must be provided to ensure that surfaces are kept clear. Flooring should be non-slip, smooth, water resistant and easy to clean. Carpets are not recommended due to the possibility of spillages or contamination by bodily fluids. Walls and ceilings should also be smooth, durable and easy to clean, and any structural damage should be attended to immediately.

Waste Management

All healthcare waste must be stored in a secure and cleanable area, and away from possible contact with service users. Staff must be trained in correct segregation and disposal of healthcare waste, and local policy must be adhered to all times.

Food and Water

Food and water are also potential sources of contamination for vulnerable groups. Food preparation areas must be designed in a manner that allows correct storage and segregation of different food types. An adequate number of wash hand basins must be available and these must not be used for washing of utensils or food preparation. Cleaning schedules must be in place and staff must be trained in correct hygiene protocol when working with food.

An adequate supply of potable water must be available for drinking, washing vegetables and making ice. Water from the storage tank may be contaminated by dust, debris or pests, and must not be used for these purposes.

Role of the Healthcare Assistant in Preventing the Spread of Infection

The healthcare assistant plays a vital role in the prevention of spread of infection within the healthcare environment. Adherence to local policy on infection control is essential to ensure that the healthcare assistant does not become a vehicle for the transfer of pathogenic micro-organisms from one client to another during the course of their duties. In order to maintain the highest standards and to reduce the likelihood of the spread of HCAIs, the healthcare assistant must strictly adhere to:

1. Good personal hygiene.

2. Correct hand washing technique.

3. Waste management policy (segregation, storage and disposal of risk and non-risk waste).

4. Handling and disposal of sharps policy.

5. Needle stick injury policy.

6. Correct segregation of linen (clean/dirty/infected).

7. Correct use and disposal of PPE.

8. Attendance of infection control training on a regular basis or as directed by the infection control nurse.

9. Reporting of any illnesses that may impact on client health status.

10. Uniforms policy.

Revision Questions

1. Outline the role and function of the infection control team.

2. List two rights/powers of the safety representative.

3. List three ways in which the built environment can contribute to the spread of infection in a healthcare setting.

4. Explain how heating and ventilation systems can harbour harmful micro-organisms.

5. State three requirements for internal walls and ceilings in a healthcare environment.

6. Briefly explain how the healthcare assistant can help prevent the spread of infection while carrying out their daily tasks.

Appendixes

Appendix 1 Cleaning Method Statements

Damp Dusting

In order to control dispersal of dust, and in line with NHO/HSE guidelines (2006) on cleaning for acute hospitals, only damp dusting is to be carried out in healthcare environments. **Dry dusting is strictly prohibited.**

Damp dusting is to be carried out on the following surfaces:

- Residents' beds
- Residents' trolleys
- Bedside lockers
- Equipment trolleys
- Cleaning equipment.

Equipment Required

Colour-coded bucket

Colour-coded cloth

Colour-coded gloves

Cleaning trolley

General purpose detergent or general surface cleaner

Health and Safety

Refer to in-house policy for guidance on all cleaning processes, colour coding, equipment, protective clothing, fluids and methods.

Never mix cleaning agents as poisonous gases could result (refer to manufacturers' instructions).

Do not climb on furniture or overreach.

All equipment should be left clean, dry and tidy in the storage area after use.

Method

1. Wash hands and put on gloves.

2. Prepare the cleaning solution in a well-ventilated area (always refer to manufacturer's instructions).

3. Place the bucket onto a cleaning trolley.

4. Dampen or rinse a cloth in the cleaning solution.

5. Remove items from the surface to be cleaned.

6. To damp dust flat surfaces, wipe in straight lines, cleaning the edges first.

7. If cleaning a bedside table, move it out and wipe underneath.

8. Wipe the main surfaces in a figure-of-eight (8) pattern.

9. **Note**: Frequently turn the cloth and rinse it in the cleaning solution. Change the cleaning solution when it becomes soiled.

10. Use the chosen cleaning solution to remove any grease marks or stubborn stains.

11. Replace items onto the clean surface.

12. After use, all equipment should be checked, cleaned, dried and returned to the storage area. Dispose of cloth or return for laundering as appropriate.

Source: Health Service Executive 2006

Dust Control – Mop Sweeping

Due to the likelihood of the dispersal of dust, **sweeping brushes are prohibited in resident areas**. A mop sweeper (dust control device) is to be utilised at all times.

Equipment Required

Colour-coded dustpan and brush

Colour-coded dust control system

Colour-coded gloves

Warning signs

Health and Safety

Refer to in-house policy for guidance on all cleaning processes, colour coding, equipment, protective clothing, fluids and methods.

Do not ever use a sweeping brush in a patient area.

All equipment should be left clean, dry and tidy in the storage area after use.

Method

1. Wash hands and put on gloves.

2. Display the warning signs in the area, ensuring all signs are visible.

3. Attach the head to the dust control device.

4. Pick up all large items of litter e.g. crisp bags and tissues.

5. Use a scraper to remove any chewing gum from the floor area.

6. Starting with the edges, dust the area using an overlapping figure-of-eight (8) pattern.

7. Dust from the farthest point and work towards the door.

8. The head should be kept in contact with the floor at all times.

9. When the head is full, remove and return it for laundering or dispose of it accordingly.

10. Replace with a new head and continue the process.

11. Use a dustpan and brush to remove remaining particles.

12. Dispose of or return the head for laundering when the task is complete.

13. After use, all equipment should be checked, cleaned, dried and returned to the storage area.

14. Remove gloves and wash hands.

Source: Health Service Executive 2006

Flat Mopping

Equipment Required

Colour-coded bucket with compatible wringer

Colour-coded gloves

Colour-coded mop handle

Colour-coded mop head

Cleaning trolley

Dust control system

Laundry bag

Vacuum cleaner

Warning signs

Floor cleaner or general purpose detergent

Health and Safety

Refer to in-house policy for guidance on all cleaning processes, colour coding, equipment, protective clothing, fluids and methods.

Work in small sections to prevent overstretching.

Ensure that the area has been dust controlled or vacuumed first.

When mopping a corridor, mop half first leaving a clearly identified dry area for patients/clients/visitors to walk on.

Do not over-wet the floor.

If mopping stairs, ensure that the area is cordoned off and warning signs are displayed.

All equipment should be left clean, dry and tidy in the storage area after use.

Method

1. Wash hands and put on gloves.

2. Display the warning signs in the area, ensuring all signs are visible.

3. Control dust the floor or vacuum clean.

4. Prepare the cleaning solution in a well-ventilated area (always refer to manufacturer's instructions).

5. Attach head to the mop handle.

6. Submerge the mop into the cleaning solution and remove excess solution from the mop in the wringer.

7. Mop the floor in 1–2 metre squared sections.

8. Mop the edges of the floor with a straight stroke, cleaning the rest of the section using a figure-of-eight (8) pattern. Leave the floor as dry as possible after.

9. Avoid splashing other surfaces and remove any splashes that do occur.

10. **Note**: Regularly replace the mop head and replace the water as appropriate.

11. On completion, remove mop head and place in a laundry bag for laundering.

12. After use, all equipment should be checked, cleaned, dried and returned to the storage area.

13. Remove gloves and wash hands.

Source: Health Service Executive 2006

Sanitary Cleaning – Toilet Cleaning

Equipment Required

Colour-coded bucket

Colour-coded cloths

Colour-coded gloves

Colour-coded labelled spray bottle

Non-abrasive pad

Supply of toilet paper (to replenish stock)

Toilet brush

Warning signs

General surface cleaner/toilet cleaner

Health and Safety

Refer to in-house policy for guidance on all cleaning processes, colour coding, equipment, protective clothing, fluids and methods.

Never mix cleaning agents as poisonous gases could result (refer to manufacturers' instructions).

Do not splash walls and fixtures.

Do not scratch surfaces with abrasive items as scratches may harbour harmful bacteria.

Report faults and damages to the supervisor.

Ensure warning signs are displayed.

All equipment should be left clean, dry and tidy in the storage area after use.

Method

1. Wash hands and put on gloves.

2. Assemble the equipment and check for safety.

3. Display the warning signs in the area, ensuring all signs are visible.

4. Prepare the cleaning solution in a well-ventilated area (always refer to manufacturer's instructions).

5. Ventilate the cleaning area to be cleaned (e.g. open a window).

6. Flush the toilet with the seat lid down.

7. Using the toilet brush, lower the water level by pushing the water back down the U-bend to expose the waterline.

8. Apply the cleaning agent to the inside of the bowl, including under the rims, and allow to soak (leave the toilet brush in the bowl).

9. Remove any splashes or marks from the wall.

10. Dampen or rinse a cloth in the cleaning solution and wring it out well.

11. Start cleaning at the highest point and work towards the lowest, from outside to inside and from clean to dirty.

12. Wipe outside and around the toilet bowl; pipe work; cistern; underneath, top and hinges of the toilet seat lid; and sanitary bins.

13. Scrub the toilet bowl and its rims with the toilet brush, particularly any stains and waterlines.

14. Flush the toilet, rinsing the brush in flushing water.

15. Wipe the brush holder and replace the brush.

16. Wipe the toilet seat. Flush the handle using the cloth then close the lid.

17. Check and replenish toilet paper if necessary.

18. Dispose of the cloth (refer to local policy) when the task is complete.

19. After use, all equipment should be checked, cleaned, dried and returned to the storage area.

20. Remove gloves and wash hands.

Source: Health Service Executive 2006

Sanitary Cleaning – Wash Hand Basins

Equipment Required

Colour-coded bucket or colour-coded labelled spray bottle

Colour-coded cloth

Colour-coded gloves

Bottlebrush

Non-abrasive pad

Pair of tweezers

Supply of soaps, paper towels and waste bags (to replenish stock)

Warning signs

General purpose detergent, general surface cleaner or bath/washbasin/shower/bidet cleaner.

Health and Safety

Refer to in-house policy for guidance on all cleaning processes, colour coding, equipment, protective clothing, fluids and methods.

Never mix cleaning agents as poisonous gases could result (refer to manufacturers' instructions).

Throughout the cleaning, regularly clean the cloth and rinse it in cleaning solution.

Do not scratch surfaces with abrasive items as scratches may harbour harmful bacteria.

Report faults, for example cracked/broken items or any build-up of scale, to your supervisor.

Display warning signs and ensure that they are clearly visible.

All equipment should be left clean, dry and tidy in the storage area after use.

Method

1. Wash hands and put on gloves.

2. Display the warning signs in the area, ensuring all signs are visible.

3. Prepare the cleaning solution in a well-ventilated area (refer to manufacturer's instructions).

4. Ventilate the area to be cleaned (e.g. open a window).

5. Remove any objects from the basin (e.g. the patient's personal items).

6. Remove any hair or other items from the plug, plughole and plug chain with the tweezers.

7. Dampen or rinse a cloth in the cleaning solution and wring it out well.

8. Start cleaning from outside and work towards the inside.

9. Wipe the surrounding surfaces of the bowl, including wall tiles, ledges, pipes, underneath the basin, paper towel dispenser and soap dispenser.

10. Wipe the inside of the bowl, including the plug, plughole, plug chain and taps, with a cloth rinsed and wrung out in the cleaning solution.

11. With running tap water, rinse the basin thoroughly, directing water into the overflow. Clean the overflow with a bottlebrush.

12. Polish stainless steel or chrome.

13. Replace items to original position, replenish soap and paper towels.

14. Dispose of the cloth (refer to local policy) when the task is complete.

15. After use, all equipment should be checked, cleaned, dried and returned to the storage area.

16. Remove gloves and wash hands.

Source: Health Service Executive 2006

Sanitary Cleaning – Bath

Equipment Required

Colour-coded bucket or colour-coded labelled spray bottle

Colour-coded cloth

Colour-coded gloves

Bottlebrush

Non-abrasive pad/cloth

Pair of tweezers

Supply of soaps, paper towels and waste bags (to replenish stock)

Warning signs

General purpose detergent, general surface cleaner or bath/washbasin/shower/bidet cleaner

Health and Safety

Refer to in-house policy for guidance on all cleaning processes, colour coding, equipment, protective clothing, fluids and methods.

Never mix cleaning agents as poisonous gases could result (refer to manufacturers' instructions).

Throughout the cleaning, regularly clean the cloth and rinse it in cleaning solution.

Do not scratch surfaces with abrasive items as scratches may harbour harmful bacteria.

Report faults, for example cracked/broken items or any build-up of scale, to the supervisor.

Display warning signs and ensure that they are clearly visible.

All equipment should be left clean, dry and tidy in the storage area after use.

Method

1. Wash hands and put on gloves.

2. Display the warning signs in the area, ensuring all signs are visible.

3. Prepare the cleaning solution in a well-ventilated area (refer to manufacturer's instructions).

4. Ventilate the area to be cleaned (e.g. open a window).

5. Remove any objects from the bath (e.g. soap).

6. Remove any hair or other items from the plug, plughole and plug chain with the tweezers.

7. Dampen or rinse a cloth in the cleaning solution and wring it out well. Start cleaning from the outside and work towards the inside.

8. Wipe the surrounding surfaces of the bath, including wall tiles, ledges, pipes, underneath the bath, paper towel dispenser and soap dispenser.

9. Polish stainless steel or chrome with the cloth.

10. Wipe the inside of the bath, including the plug, plughole, plug chain, taps and overflow.

11. With running tap water, rinse the bath thoroughly, directing water into the overflow. Clean the overflow with a bottlebrush.

12. To remove any build-up of soap and grease, apply the cleaning solution and use a non-abrasive pad.

13. Remove any splashes or marks from the walls and wipe door handles.

14. Dispose of the cloth (refer to local policy) when the task is complete.

15. After use, all equipment should be checked, cleaned, dried and returned to the storage area.

16. Remove gloves and wash hands.

Source: Health Service Executive 2006

Sanitary Cleaning – Shower Room

Equipment Required

Colour-coded bucket or colour-coded labelled spray bottle

Colour-coded cloth

Colour-coded gloves

Bottlebrush

Non-abrasive pad

Pair of tweezers

Warning signs

General purpose detergent, general surface cleaner or bath/washbasin/shower/bidet cleaner

Health and Safety

Refer to in-house policy for guidance on all cleaning processes, colour coding, equipment, protective clothing, fluids and methods.

Never mix cleaning agents as poisonous gases could result (refer to manufacturers' instructions).

Throughout the cleaning operation, regularly clean the cloth and rinse it in cleaning solution.

Do not scratch surfaces with abrasive items as scratches may harbour harmful bacteria.

Report faults, for example cracked/broken items or any build-up of scale, to the supervisor.

Display warning signs and ensure that they are clearly visible.

All equipment should be left clean, dry and tidy in the storage area after use.

Method

1. Wash hands and put on gloves.

2. Display the warning signs in the area, ensuring all signs are visible.

3. Prepare the cleaning solution in a well-ventilated area (refer to manufacturer's instructions).

4. Ventilate the area to be cleaned (e.g. open a window).

5. Empty waste bins.

6. Remove any hair or other items from the plug, plughole and plug chain with the tweezers.

7. Dampen or rinse a cloth in the cleaning solution and wring it out well.

8. Start cleaning at the highest point and work towards the lowest, from outside to inside and from clean to dirty.

9. Clean the curtain rail. Then starting at the highest point of the shower, wipe the wall tiles from clean to dirty areas.

10. Check the shower curtain – wipe clean and dry; change if necessary.

11. Wipe the showerhead, hose, taps and soap tray.

12. If a shower tray is present, clean the inside with a wrung-out cloth.

13. Wipe around the inside of the shower cubicle.

14. Clean the overflow with a bottlebrush.

15. To remove any build-up of soap and grease, apply cleaning solution and use a non-abrasive pad.

16. Rinse the shower cubicle thoroughly with clean water, swilling the water into the overflow.

17. Where rubber mats are present, thoroughly clean and dry (e.g. by airing).

18. Polish stainless steel or chrome.

19. Dispose of the cloth (refer to local policy) when the task is complete.

20. After use, all equipment should be checked, cleaned, dried and returned to the storage area.

21. Remove gloves and wash hands.

Source: Health Service Executive 2006

Appendix 2 Management of Blood and Other Bodily Fluid Spillages: Policy and Procedure

According to the HSE (2011), occupational exposure to blood, other bodily fluids, secretions and excretions through spillages pose a potential risk of infection, particularly to those who may be exposed while providing health and social care. The safe and effective management of such spillages is, therefore, essential in order to prevent transmission of infection via this route, and for health and safety in general.

In the event of a spillage, gather the necessary equipment listed below:

1. Personal protective equipment – gloves (essential), goggles and mask.

2. An apron or gown should be worn if there is a risk of splashing to eyes, mouth and/or body.

3. Waste receptacle – check that the correct waste bag is available e.g. yellow for healthcare risk waste.

4. Items to manage the spillage – disposable paper towels, disinfectant, spillage kit etc.

5. Single-incident use disposable scoops.

Note: Personal protective equipment must be worn.

In the first instance, containment of spillages may be necessary. This should be done using disposable towels. If the spillage is large, first use disposable towels to absorb/contain the fluid. Care must be taken to avoid splashing during this time, especially as the spillage has not yet been inactivated with disinfectant.

Hard Surfaces

1. Apply an approved disinfectant to the spillage, ensuring that the spillage is completely covered and towels are completely saturated.

2. Approved disinfectants should be those containing a solution or granules of sodium hypochlorite or sodium dichloroisocyanurate, with a concentration of 10,000 ppm available chlorine (av).

3. Manufacturers' instructions should be followed to ensure that correct contact time is achieved (usually a few minutes).

4. Use clean towels/disinfectant on the area, cleaning upwards from the area and placing disposable towels immediately into a healthcare risk waste receptacle. This receptacle should be close to hand for doing this immediately and safely.

5. Never leave these contaminated towels on any other surface.

6. The area should then be further cleaned using fresh disposable towels and a solution of water and general purpose detergent.

7. All remaining items used should finally be disposed of into a healthcare risk waste receptacle.

8. If reusable equipment is used (e.g. buckets and mop heads), it must be cleaned/laundered, dried and stored appropriately.

9. Personal protective equipment worn should then be removed and disposed of into the waste stream.

10. Hand hygiene should be performed after.

Soft Furnishings

1. Where soft furnishings have been used/are in place during delivery of care, the steps described above for managing hard surfaces can be applied.

2. For those items that may become damaged by this process (i.e. use of disinfectants), a solution of detergent and water can be used to clean the area thoroughly.

3. Soft furnishings can also be wet vacuumed.

4. Following the cleaning of soft furnishings, every effort must be made to air the room to allow drying before reuse.

Chlorine-releasing agents, such as those described above inactivate blood-borne viruses. The concentration described represents a 1:10 dilution of household bleach; however, strengths of brands can differ and deterioration may occur during storage. Alcohol solutions should not be used to clear spillages.

Good Practice Points

1. Spillages should be dealt with immediately.

2. All necessary equipment to deal with a spillage must first be gathered, including personal protective equipment and spillage kits.

3. Appropriate solutions must be used for the safe and effective management of spillages.

4. All items used during a spillage must be disposed of or cleaned appropriately.

5. Hand hygiene should be performed following management of spillages.

6. Safety data sheets should also be referred to so as to ensure safe management of spillages.

7. Responsibilities for the cleaning of blood and bodily fluid spillages must be clearly documented.

8. All healthcare workers who may be exposed to spillages of blood or bodily fluids must receive training in the safe and effective management of blood or other bodily fluid spillages.

9. Training records must be held to reflect this.

Source: Health Service Executive 2006

Bibliography

Centers for Disease Control and Prevention, 'Healthcare-Associated Infections' (2012), available online at: http://www.cdc.gov/phlp/publications/topic/hai.html

Department of Health and Children, *Segregation, Packaging and Storage Guidelines for Healthcare Risk Waste, Third Edition* (Dublin: Hospital Planning Office, 2004)

Department of Public Health HSE East, *Community Infection Prevention and Control Manual* (Dublin: Health Service Executive, 2011)

European Parliament and Council/European Communities, Regulation (EC) No. 852/2004 on the Hygiene of Foodstuffs

Health Information and Quality Authority, *National Standards for the Prevention and Control of Healthcare Associated Infections* (Dublin: HIQA, 2009)

Health Service Executive, 'Hand Hygiene in Irish Healthcare Settings' (2013), available online at: www.hse.ie/eng/services/healthpromotion/handhygiene

Health Service Executive, *Standard Precautions* (Dublin: HSE, 2007)

National Hospitals Office/Health Service Executive, *Cleaning Manual – Acute Hospitals* (Dublin: National Hospitals Office, 2006)

Office of the Attorney General, Safety, Health and Welfare at Work Act 2005, available online at: www.irishstatute.ie

Office of the Attorney General, Safety, Health and Welfare at Work (General Application) Regulations 1993, available online at: http://www.irishstatutebook.ie/1993/en/si/0044.html

SARI, *Guidelines for Hand Hygiene in Irish Health Care Settings* (Dublin: Health Protection Surveillance Centre, HSE, 2005)

SARI, *The Control and Prevention of MRSA in Hospitals and in the Community* (Dublin: Health Protection Surveillance Centre, HSE, 2001)

Sligo General Hospital, 'Infection Prevention and Control Department' (2012), available online at: www.hse.ie/eng/services/Find_a_Service/hospitals/sligo/Hospital_Departments/Infection_Prevention_and_Control.html

Wilson, J., *Clinical Microbiology: An Introduction for Healthcare Professionals* (Beijing: Elsevier, 2008)